# Love that!
# BRENDA NOVAK'S
## every occasion cookbook

by
*New York Times* Bestselling Author

## Brenda Novak

and co-authored by Jan Coad

*[signature: Brenda Novak]*

*Cooking is like love. It should be*
*entered into with abandon or not at all.*
*—Harriet Van Horne*

# Dedication

To all those who have supported Brenda Novak's Annual Online Auction for Diabetes Research. Together, we've raised $2.4 million, far exceeding my initial hopes and even my early dreams. I couldn't be more grateful.

And to Thad and anyone else who's ever struggled with food choices and trying to improve his or her eating habits...

# Introduction

This book has been a dream of mine for several years—since my best friend first suggested I do one. I write novels for a living (over 50 so far) and yet this cookbook was probably the hardest thing I've ever created. It was hard because I wanted it to be perfect. I know that what some people can eat, others can't. So I labored most over what to include and not to include.

The struggle was worth it, however. Those who know me best understand how important it is to me that we find a cure for diabetes. My youngest son suffers from this disease, and like most mothers, I'd confront anything that ever threatened him or my other children. Sadly, I can't save him from this relentless disease. I can only fight for a cure, so that someday he—and the millions of others who suffer with him—will be free from this deadly taskmaster. That's why I've made raising money for diabetes research my life's work, along with my writing.

I hope you enjoy the meals these recipes will help you create as much as my family and I enjoy them on a daily basis!

-Brenda Novak

# Acknowledgements

Thanks to fellow author Jan Coad for contributing so many of her great recipes. Thanks, too, to Mark Casale, executive chef of Dos Coyotes Restaurants and fellow diabetes advocate, for sharing some of his delicious recipes, which we've used at our house over and over these past several years. I also owe a debt of gratitude to Lara Elizabeth Johnson MS, PA-C RD, who generously donated her time to calculate nutritional information for many of my own recipes. And last, but not least, I couldn't have completed this project without Alexa Novak, my middle daughter, who devoted so much of her time to cooking, staging, photographing the food (and cleaning up some of my personal recipes, which were, more often than not, written on tattered old recipe cards with only partial instructions) and designing the book. What a great team. I love you all.

Thank you for purchasing this book. By doing so, you have contributed to the fight against diabetes, as all the proceeds are going to fund cure-focused research at the University of Miami's Diabetes Research Foundation. I've chosen the DRI because they are the facility I feel is closest to clearing the hurdles that remain in eradicating this disease.

Here's to making a difference!

## A note from my co-author...

I am the granddaughter of a juvenile diabetic and daughter of an adult onset diabetic. I've already lost both of these men so I hope a cure is found in the near future. Also, our teenage son had an episode of acute pancreatitis, which gives him a higher risk of developing diabetes. He needs to eat a low fat diet, so we watch our fat, carbohydrate and sugar intake.

My husband and I are both avid cooks and former creator/owners of a restaurant, so we enjoy food that tastes good, is pleasing to the eye, and is balanced nutritionally to help us live healthy lives. Living in the Pacific Northwest has afforded us access to fruits and vegetables year round. I shop locally for seasonal produce and then create tasty meals.

I've enjoyed supporting Brenda's efforts to raise money for diabetes research for a few years and was very excited to help with this project. I hope you enjoy these recipes from our families to yours.

-Jan Coad

# Table of Contents

# Simple Salads

There is no
sincerer love than the
love of food.
—George Bernard
Shaw

# Pomegranate Salad

Each Serving: Cal: 353 Carb: 4.8 g Fat: 37 g Protein: 3.8 g Sodium: 59 mg Sugar: 4.8 g

3/4 c. pine nuts
1 lg. pomegranate or 1/2 c. dried cranberries
4 bunches watercress, stemmed
4 heads red leaf lettuce
Dressing:
3/4 c. olive oil
1 Tbps. raspberry vinegar
1 Tbsp. fresh lemon juice
2 Tbsp. red wine vinegar

Clean and tear the red leaf lettuce. Toss red leaf lettuce with the watercress, pomegranate seeds or cranberries and pine nuts.

Whisk together all ingredients for the dressing. Salt and pepper to taste. Shake well before pouring.

8 Servings

Salads

# Salmon Stacks

Each Serving: Cal: 371 Carb: 18 g Fat: 18 g Protein: 36 g Sodium: 236 mg Sugar: 2 g

Salads

4, 6-ounce salmon fillets
1/4 cup light balsamic vinaigrette
2 cups romaine lettuce
1/2 cucumber, peeled and thinly sliced
1 avocado, thinly sliced
1 carrot, thinly sliced
4 Tbsp. light balsamic vinaigrette

Place salmon fillets in a resealable plastic bag and add 1/4 cup balsamic vinaigrette. Allow the fillets to marinate for ten minutes.

Grill salmon fillets for 4 minutes on each side or until cooked through. On four plates, mound the lettuce, top with a salmon fillet, some cucumber slices, avocado slices and carrot slices. Drizzle with a tablespoon of the balsamic vinaigrette.

4 Servings

*The flaky salmon, soft avocado and crispiness from the carrot and cucumber adds delightful textural variety to this lunch or dinner treat.*
-Jan

# Bacon, Lettuce & Tomato Salad

Each Serving: Cal: 391 Carb: 14 g Fat: 35 g Protein: 8 g Sodium: 362 mg Sugar: 2 g

1 large ripe
avocado, cubed
1/3 lb. bacon
(12 thin strips)
cooked crispy
and chopped
1 large heirloom
tomato, chopped
2 cups mixed
greens
Dressing:
1/4 cup lemon
juice
1/4 cup extra
virgin olive oil
1/4 cup balsamic
vinegar
1/2 Tbsp. fresh
chopped basil

Prepare the vegetables, by peeling and slicing each. Place in a salad bowl. Toss with mixed greens.

Whisk together all ingredients for dressing except the olive oil, which you will whisk in at the end. Toss dressing with the salad and serve.

4 Servings

Salads

# Caprese Pasta Salad

Each Serving: Cal: 270 Carb: 36.1 g Fat: 6.6 g Protein: 15.6 g Sodium: 390 mg Sugar: 2 g

1 lb. orzo pasta
1 medium red bell pepper, diced
1 small purple onion, diced
8 oz. fresh mozzarella, cubed
1 pt. grape tomatoes, chopped
2 Tbsp. basil, chopped
Marinade/Tomato Dressing:
1/4 cup white wine vinegar
1 Tbsp. Dijon-style mustard
1/4 cup finely chopped fresh basil
1/2 tsp. salt
1/4 tsp. pepper
1/2 cup + 2 Tbsp. olive oil
2 plum tomatoes seeded & chopped

Whisk together dressing ingredients, cover and chill.

Cook pasta according to package. Drain well. Add half of the dressing while pasta is still warm. Allow it to cool and then toss with all other ingredients, reserving the basil for garnish.

8 Servings

*Note: If you're in a hurry, you can use store-bought Italian dressing instead and it's just as delicious.*
*-Brenda*

*Family favorite*

# Mandarin Almond Salad

Each Serving: Cal: 268 Carb: 16 g Fat: 21 g Protein: 7 g Sodium: 218 mg Sugar: 11 g

Salads

2 heads of butter
lettuce
2 green onions
1 cup mandarin
oranges
2 celery stalks,
sliced
1 cup almonds,
slivered
Dressing:
1/4 cup oil
1 Tbsp. honey
2 Tbsp. vinegar
1/2 tsp. salt
Dash of pepper

Tear lettuce and toss with almonds, mandarin oranges, onions and celery.

Whisk together dressing ingredients, and chill. Shake well before serving.

4 Servings

*Family favorite*

# King Crab, Green Apple, and Avocado Salad

Each Serving: Cal: 67 Carb: 6 g Fat: 4 g Protein: 4 g Sodium: 157 mg Sugar: 3 g

1 lb. king crab meat
2 green apples, cored and chopped
1 avocado, cubed
Dressing:
1/2 cup white wine vinegar
1/4 cup balsamic vinegar
Juice of one lime
1 tsp. lime zest
1/4 tsp. sea salt
1/4 tsp. white pepper
2 Tbsp. olive oil

Toss chopped apple, cubed avocado and crab meat with the dressing. Divide among 4 chilled bowls.

4 Servings

Salads

# Citrus Salad with Avocado and Bacon

Each Serving: Cal: 464 Carb: 15.6 g Fat: 46.4 g Protein: 3 g Sodium: 243 mg Sugar: 6.1 g

4 cups chopped romaine hearts
2 cups mixed baby greens
1 navel orange
1 California avocado
6 thin slices bacon, cooked, and crumbled
1/8 red onion, chopped
Citrus Vinaigrette Dressing:
2/3 cup extra-virgin olive oil
Juice of one orange
Juice of one lemon
Juice of one lime

Whisk together all dressing ingredients.

Place chopped romaine hearts and baby greens in a mixing bowl and toss with the dressing. Peel the orange and separate the sections–cutting each segment in half.

Arrange oranges, sliced avocado, crumbled bacon and chopped red onions on top.

4 Servings

# Cauliflower, Broccoli and Cheese Salad

Each Serving: Cal: 345 Carb: 10 g Fat: 30 g Protein: 12 g Sodium: 378 mg Sugar: 2 g

1 head cauliflower, cut florets
1 head broccoli, cut florets
1/4 cup mayonnaise
8 oz. cream cheese
16 oz. sour cream
1/2 tsp. salt
1/2 tsp. pepper
2 cloves garlic, chopped
2 cups cheddar cheese, shredded
1/2 cup onion, chopped

In a mixing bowl, using an electric mixer, combine mayonnaise, cream cheese and sour cream until smooth. Add salt, pepper and garlic puree and mix well.

In a large bowl, combine cauliflower, broccoli, shredded cheese and onion. Fold in dressing mix and serve.

10 Servings

*Note: By switching to low-fat mayonnaise and cheddar cheese and fat-free cream cheese and sour cream-each serving's calories are reduced to 145 and fat to 3 g.*

# Tomato & Basil Salad

Each Serving: Cal: 75 Carb: 8 g Fat: 4 g Protein: 3 g Sodium: 61 mg Sugar: 6 g

2 large tomatoes, deseeded and chopped
1/2 cucumber, peeled, deseeded and chopped
1/4 cup low-fat buttermilk
1/2 cup low-fat sour cream
3 Tbsp. fresh basil, thinly sliced
2 cloves garlic, minced

Put the cucumbers and tomatoes in a medium-sized bowl. In another bowl, mix the buttermilk, sour cream, basil and garlic.

Drizzle the dressing over the vegetables and toss.

4 Servings

Salads

# Fresh Fruit Parfait Salad

Each Serving: Cal: 148 Carb: 27 g Fat: 1 g Protein: 13 g Sodium: 42 mg Sugar: 20 g

2 peaches, diced
2 kiwi, peeled and sliced
1 cup blueberries
1 lemon, juiced and zested for garnish
1 navel orange, juiced and zested for garnish
1 lime, juiced and zested for garnish
2 cups plain Greek yogurt

In a medium-sized bowl, place cut fruit and blueberries and gently toss together. In a small bowl, stir 2 cups of non-fat plain yogurt with the lemon, orange and lime juice.

In clear glasses, layer the ingredients, starting with the fruit mixture. Next, layer with yogurt, then fruit, then yogurt. Repeat these steps until you have filled the glasses. Garnish with fruit zest.

4 Servings

# Berry Salad

Each Serving: Cal: 439 Carb: 32 g Fat: 32 g Protein: 10g Sodium: 794 mg Sugar: 22 g

2 cups strawberries
1 cup raspberries
1 cup blackberries
spring salad mix
1 cup pecans, chopped
blue cheese crumbles
Dressing:
2 Tbsp. apple cider vinegar
1/4 cup white sugar
1/2 cup plain Greek yogurt
1 tsp. salt
1 tsp. onion powder
2 Tbsp. vegetable oil
3 tsp. poppy seeds

In a mixing bowl, toss together the spring salad mix, raspberries, blackberries, sliced strawberries, chopped pecans and blue cheese crumbles.

Blend all dressing ingredients together, except for the poppy seeds. Pour into a small mixing bowl and stir in poppy seeds. Let dressing chill in refrigerator before serving.

4 Servings

*Family favorite*

# Broccoli Salad

Each Serving: Cal: 195 Carb: 17.4 g Fat: 12.9 g Protein: 4.3 g Sodium: 320 mg Sugar: 9.8 g

10 slices bacon
1 head broccoli,
cut florets
1/4 cup red
onion, chopped
1/2 cup raisins
3 Tbsp. white
wine vinegar
2 Tbsp. honey
1 cup
mayonnaise
1/4 cup
sunflower seeds
2 Tbsp. extra-
virgin olive oil
1 tsp. chopped
fresh thyme

Cook bacon in the microwave until crispy, then crumble. Combine broccoli, onion and raisins in a large mixing bowl. In a small bowl, whisk together the vinegar, honey and mayonnaise. Pour over broccoli mixture. Add the bacon and toss until well mixed.

Refrigerate before serving.

6 Servings

*Family favorite*

# Pasta Salad

Each Serving: Cal: 160 Carb: 13 g Fat: 9 g Protein: 7 g Sodium: 403 mg Sugar: 2 g

1 cup small shells pasta
2 cups zucchini, grated
2 cloves garlic, thinly sliced and made into a paste by smashing
3 Tbsp. extra-virgin olive oil
3 Tbsp. balsamic vinegar
1/4 tsp. red pepper flakes
1/4 tsp. sea salt
1/4 tsp. ground black pepper
1/4 lb. thinly sliced Black Forest ham, cut into strips
1/2 cup crumbled feta cheese
1 1/2 Tbsp. fresh parsley, chopped
1 1/2 Tbsp. fresh cilantro, chopped

Boil the pasta (add a pinch of salt to the water). Trim and peel zucchini, then grate into a bowl. Add salt, toss and let sit for 10 minutes. Squeeze any excess moisture out of zucchini.

In a large bowl, mix garlic, red pepper flakes, olive oil and balsamic vinegar. Whisk together to mix well. Add remaining ingredients and toss with the pasta. Chill before serving to combine the flavors.

8 Servings

*Family favorite*

# Summer Corn and Tomato Salad

Each Serving: Cal: 119 Carb: 21 g Fat: 3 g Protein: 5 g Sodium: 58 mg Sugar: 6 g

6 ears fresh corn, husked
4 cups grape-tomatoes
1/2 red onion, diced
1 cup cooked black beans
1 jalapeno pepper, chopped
1/4 cup cilantro, chopped
Juice of 1 lime
1 Tbsp. red wine vinegar
2 Tbsp. olive oil
1/2 tsp. salt
1/4 tsp. pepper

Bring a big pot of salted water to boil. Add the corn and immediately turn off the heat. Cover for 3-5 minutes, until the corn is crunchy tender. Drain and cool.

Cut corn kernels from the cob with a sharp knife. Toss the corn with the remaining ingredients. You may serve spooned over a bed of salad greens.

12 Servings

*Note: The nutritional information is figured without the salad greens.*

*Family favorite*

# The Salad Blues

Each Serving: Cal: 119 Carb: 21 g Fat: 3 g Protein: 5 g Sodium: 58 mg Sugar: 6 g

1 Tbsp. chives, chopped
2 heads romaine hearts, chopped
2 cups blueberries
1 cup blue cheese crumbles
Dressing:
2 Tbsp. balsamic vinegar
2 Tbsp. sugar free blueberry syrup
1 tsp. extra-virgin olive oil
1 tsp. Dijon mustard

Toss together chives, chopped lettuce, blueberries, and blue cheese.

Whisk together all dressing ingredients and toss to serve.

6 Servings

*Blueberries and blue cheese are great together in this salad. I love hearts of romaine, so I mix up the salad and serve it inside a nice large leaf of lettuce.*
*-Jan*

Salads

# Easy Homemade Soups

"Soup puts the heart at ease, eliminates the tension of the day and awakens and refines the appetite."
-Auguste Escoffier

# Mediterranean Vegetable Soup

Each Serving: Cal: 109 Carb: 13 g Fat: 4 g Protein: 6 g Sodium: 204 mg Sugar: 6 g

2 Tbsp. olive oil
6 large ripe tomatoes, skinned, cored and halved
3 large yellow bell peppers, seeded and halved
3 zucchini, halved lengthwise
1 small eggplant
4 garlic cloves
2 onions, cut in eighths
4 cups chicken or vegetable stock
1/2 tsp. salt
1/4 tsp. pepper
1 Tbsp. shredded basil leaves to garnish

Preheat the oven to 375° F. Brush baking dish with olive oil. Lay vegetables on dish, cut side down. Tuck the garlic & onions into gaps and drizzle with remaining olive oil. Then season lightly with salt and pepper. Place in oven and bake uncovered for 30-35 minutes, until soft and browned around edges.

Slowly add batches of vegetables into a food processor and chop until consistency of salsa–do not puree. Combine the stock and chopped vegetable mixture in a saucepan and simmer over medium heat for 20-25 minutes. Taste and adjust seasoning and serve.

8 Servings

Soups

# Potato-Leek Soup

Each Serving: Cal: 322 Carb: 40.3 g Fat: 14.3 g Protein: 10.7 g Sodium: 924 mg Sugar: 12.2 g

Soups

3 Tbsp. butter
2 red onions, pureed
2 leeks, chopped
2 celery stalks, chopped
3 cups chicken stock
4 potatoes, thinly sliced
4 cups milk
1 cup half-and-half
1 tsp. salt
1/2 tsp. pepper
1/4 mace

Clean and thinly slice potatoes and leeks. Peel and puree onions. In a large pot, melt butter over medium heat, add onions and sauté for about 10 minutes. Mix in the salt, pepper and mace.

Pour in the stock and add the leeks and celery. Let cook for about 15 minutes. Add potatoes, reduce heat, cook and let simmer until potatoes are done, about 20 minutes. Blend half of the soup in blender and then return to pot. Pour in milk and half-and-half and let simmer for about 10 minutes.

6 Servings

*Family favorite*

# Cream of Cauliflower

Each Serving: Cal: 419 Carb: 16.5 g Fat: 30 g Protein: 22.4 g Sodium: 1146 mg Sugar: 6.9 g

4 Tbsp. butter
1 large red onion, pureed
2 tsp. garlic, chopped
1/4 cup flour
4 cups chicken broth
1 cup milk
2 cups half-and- half
2 pounds cauliflower
1 1/2 tsp. Dijon mustard
2 cups cheddar cheese, shredded
1 cup pepper jack cheese, shredded
1 tsp. salt
1 tsp. pepper

Clean and break apart cauliflower. Peel and puree onion and garlic. In a large pot, melt butter over medium heat. Add onion and garlic and sauté for about 5 minutes. Mix in flour. Pour in milk, half-and-half and broth, stirring constantly.

Add cauliflower and heat to a boil. Reduce heat, cover and let simmer for about 15 minutes, until cauliflower is tender but not mushy. Place contents into a blender and puree. Return to pot and gradually stir in cheese, mustard, salt and pepper.

8 Servings

Note: The sodium content changes to 799 mg with low-sodium broth.

# Mulligatawny Soup

Each Serving: Cal: 268 Carb: 38.1 g Fat: 7.5 g Protein: 11.8 g Sodium: 729 mg Sugar: 5.8 g

Soups

1/2 c. onion, pureed
1 carrot, sliced
2 celery sticks, sliced
1/4 c. butter
1/2 Tbsp. flour
2 tsp. curry
4 c. chicken broth
1 bay leaf
2 tart apples, chopped
1/2 c. boiled rice
1 1/2 cup cubed cooked chicken
1 tsp. salt
1/4 tsp. pepper

Slice carrot and celery. Peel and puree onion. In a large pot, melt butter over medium heat. Add onion, carrot and celery. Sauté until onion is translucent but do not brown.

Stir in flour, curry, chicken broth and bay leaf and cook for 3 minutes. Add apples, boiled rice, cubed chicken, seasonings and let simmer for 15 minutes.

Before serving, stir in 1 cup cream.

8 Servings

*Family favorite*

# Chicken Tortilla Soup

Each Serving: Cal: 410 Carb: 40.1 g Fat: 12.1 g Protein: 36 g Sodium: 1377 mg Sugar: 4.2 g

Soups

2 Tbsp. butter
1 onion
4 cloves of garlic
2 jalapenos
4 chicken breasts
1/4 lime juice
6 cups chicken broth
2 cups of corn
1 can of black beans
1 can fire roasted tomatoes
1/4 tsp. chili powder
1 tsp. salt
1/2 tsp. pepper
1 cup fresh cilantro, chopped
3 flour tortillas

Puree the onion, garlic and jalapenos. Melt the butter in a large pot over low heat. Saute the onion, garlic and jalapenos for about 3 minutes. Pour the lime, chicken broth, corn, black beans and tomatoes into the pot. Bring to a boil and add chicken. Reduce heat to simmer and cook for 20-25 minutes. When chicken is fully cooked, remove from the pot and shred. Return to pot and add salt, pepper and fresh cilantro.

Preheat oven to 350° F. Cut tortillas into strips and place on a baking sheet. Sprinkle salt over strips and bake until golden brown. Use to garnish each bowl.

6 Servings

*Note: Using low-sodium broth will reduce the sodium to 684 mg.*

# Broccoli-Cheddar Soup

Each Serving: Cal: 389 Carb: 30.6 g Fat: 21.8 g Protein: 18.3 g Sodium: 1079 mg Sugar: 6.5 g

2 pounds of broccoli crowns
1/4 cup butter
1 Tbsp. curry powder
1 large purple onion, pureed
6 cups regular chicken broth
1 bouillon cube
3 large potatoes, thinly sliced
5 carrots, thinly sliced
1 cup milk
3-4 cup shredded sharp cheddar cheese

In a large pot, melt butter over medium heat. Add curry powder and onion. Sauté for about 10 minutes. Add broth, bouillon cube, potatoes and carrots.

Reduce heat, cover and let simmer for 35 minutes, stirring occasionally. Break up crowns and add flowerettes to the pot. Let simmer for 5 more minutes. Scoop half of the broth and vegetables into a blender and puree it. Then pour the puree back into the pot. Stir in milk and cheese.

8 Servings

*Family favorite*

*Note: Using low-sodium broth will reduce the sodium to 559 mg.*

Soups

# Beef and Vegetable Soup

Each Serving: Cal: 166 Carb: 17 g Fat: 5 g Protein: 9 g Sodium: 415 mg Sugar: 5 g

4 cups beef stock
1/2 Tbsp. fresh rosemary, chopped
1/2 Tbsp. fresh thyme, chopped
10 oz. lean sirloin or round steak
1 Tbsp. olive oil
1 large carrot, diced
2 cloves of garlic, minced
1 medium onion, diced
3 medium red potatoes, diced
2 celery stalks, sliced
1/2 cup Cabernet Sauvignon
1/2 tsp. salt
1/4 tsp. black pepper

Place the onions, carrot, and potatoes in a large pot with olive oil drizzled on the bottom of the pan. Allow the vegetables to cook until the onions are clear. Add the wine and stir to bring up the flavors from the pan. Pour in the stock and add mixed herbs. Bring to a boil, cover and simmer gently over low heat for 10 minutes.

Trim any fat from the beef and cut the meat into thin strips. Add the beef to the pan. Bring back to a boil, cover and simmer about 1 hour or until beef and vegetables are tender. Adjust seasoning to taste, ladle soup into warmed bowls, garnish with rosemary.

8 Servings

# Strawberry Soup

Each Serving: Cal: 115 Carb: 19 g Fat: 0 g Protein: 9 g Sodium: 39 mg Sugar: 15 g

3 cups of fresh strawberries
2 cups plain non-fat Greek yogurt
1 cup orange juice
1/4 cup Stevia sweetener

Put all ingredients into a food processor or blender and mix until smooth. May garnish with whipped topping and a strawberry.

6 servings

# Red Pepper Soup

Each Serving: Cal: 115 Carb: 12 g Fat: 5 g Protein: 7 g Sodium: 437 mg Sugar: 6 g

2 Tbsp. olive oil
3 red bell peppers, chopped
1/2 large fennel bulb, chopped
1 small onion, chopped
4 cups chicken stock
1 cup plain non-fat Greek yogurt
1/2 tsp. sea salt
1/2 tsp. white pepper
1/2 tsp. cayenne pepper

In large pot, heat olive oil and cook red peppers, fennel and onion until softened, about 15 minutes. Add chicken broth and bring to a boil over high heat. Reduce heat to medium and simmer for 20 minutes.

Work in small batches–puree soup until smooth. Add the yogurt with the last batch. Return the soup to the pot and heat through. Do not bring to a boil or the yogurt will curdle. Garnish each bowl with a swirl of yogurt and fresh basil.

6 servings

Soups

# Chunky Chicken Vegetable Soup

Each Serving: Cal: 201 Carb: 18 g Fat: 4 g Protein: 20 g Sodium: 141 mg Sugar: 4 g

1 Tbsp. olive oil
2 carrots, sliced
1 onion, diced
2 garlic cloves, crushed
3 medium potatoes, peeled and diced
2 celery stalks, sliced
6 large tomatoes, peeled and chopped
2 1/2 cups chicken stock
1 bay leaf
1 Tbsp. fresh basil, chopped
1 Tbsp. fresh rosemary, chopped
2 cups cooked chicken breast, chopped
1/2 cup green cabbage, shredded

Place the carrots, onions, garlic, potatoes, celery and tomatoes in a large pan with the olive oil; cook over medium heat until the onions are clear. Add stock and stir in the bay leaf and herbs. Bring to a boil, then reduce the heat, cover and simmer for 25 minutes.

Add the corn and cabbage and return to a boil. Reduce the heat, cover and simmer for 5 more minutes or until vegetables are tender. Remove and discard the bay leaf. Ladle into warm bowls, garnish with fresh spring of basil and serve immediately.

6 Servings

Note: This one may also be eaten vegetarian by switching the chicken stock for vegetable stock and eliminating the meat.

# Albondigas Soup

Each serving: Cal: 399 Carb: 31.6 g Fat 16.6 g Protein 28.7 g, Sodium 1823 mg Sugar: 3.4 g

Soups

**Soup Base:**
1 Tbsp. vegetable oil
1/2 medium sweet onion, chopped
3 cloves garlic, minced
1/2 tsp. Mexican crushed oregano
1/2 tsp. ground cumin
2 cans 12.7 oz. crushed tomatoes
1 chipotle chili, diced
1 tsp. of adobo sauce
2 carrots, diced
2 zucchinis, diced
6 cups chicken broth
1 cup cooked white rice

**Meatballs:**
1/2 pound ground beef
4 links sweet Italian sausage, casings removed
1 egg
1 clove garlic, minced
1 cup fresh cilantro, chopped
1 cup fresh oregano, chopped
1/2 tsp. salt
1/2 tsp. ground cumin

For the soup base, sauté first five ingredients on low, being careful to not burn the garlic. Once onions are opaque, add the chipotle chili and sauce, stir, then add the carrots, stir and sauté for 3 min. Add tomatoes and chicken broth. Allow soup base to simmer while you begin making your meatballs.

For the meatballs: Mix all ingredients, form to small balls and cook in the oven at 350° F until almost cooked through. Then add meatballs, one at a time to the soup base. Cook on low for an hour. Add the zucchini and cooked rice and simmer for an additional 30 min, or until zucchini is tender. Serve with fresh chopped cilantro and diced avocado.

6 Servings

*Thank you to Rebecca Salazar for this fabulous recipe. She won the contest I ran on Facebook looking for one special contributor.*
*-Brenda*

# Creamy Carrot and Curry Soup

Each Serving: Cal: 167 Carb: 12 g Fat: 13 g Protein: 1 g Sodium: 265 mg Sugar: 5 g

1/4 cup butter
1 medium onion, chopped,
4 cups of carrots chopped
2 Tbsp. curry powder
1 Tbsp. lemon zest
3 cups chicken or vegetable stock
1/2 cup heavy cream
1/2 tsp. salt
1/4 tsp. white pepper
Sprigs of fresh cilantro, to garnish

Melt butter in a large pan over low heat. Add the onion and cook, stirring for 3 minutes, until slightly softened. Add the carrots, cover and cook, stirring occasionally, for about 5 minutes. Stir in the curry, lemon zest and stock and bring to boil. Reduce heat and simmer for 30-35 minutes, until the vegetables are tender. Remove the soup from the heat and let cool for 10 minutes.

Transfer the soup to a food processor to blend and process until smooth. Return the soup to the rinsed-out pan, stir in the cream, and season well with salt and pepper.

6 Servings

# Tomato Bisque with Alaskan King Crab

Each Serving: Cal: 381 Carb: 30.6 g Fat: 23.2 g Protein: 10.8 g Sodium: 1979 mg Sugar: 21.3 g

Soups

28 oz. can of quality Italian tomatoes
2 cups heavy cream
2 cups whole milk
2 whole carrots, chopped
2 cloves garlic, minced
1 Tbsp. salt
1/2 tsp. white pepper
1/2 tsp. cayenne pepper
1 cup king crab meat
3 Tbsp. fresh basil, chopped

Puree tomatoes, carrots and garlic in a food processor or heavy-duty blender.

Place mixture into soup pot and add heavy cream and milk. Add salt, white pepper, cayenne pepper and crab meat. Let simmer on low for half an hour. Adjust seasoning as desired. You may garnish with fresh chopped basil or croutons.

8 Servings

*Note: You can often just buy a container of fresh crab meat from Costco, which is cooked and add it at the end.*

*Family favorite*

# Market Fresh Vegetable Soup

Each Serving: Cal: 108 Carb: 17 g Fat: 4 g Protein: 4 g Sodium: 214 mg Sugar: 4 g

2 Tbsp. olive oil
1/2 onion, chopped
4 cups chicken stock
2 cups of yellow fingerling potatoes, sliced
3 large carrots, chopped
1/2 head of cauliflower, chopped
2 cups white cabbage, chopped
1/2 tsp. sea salt
1/2 tsp. pepper
2 sprigs fresh rosemary

Sauté onions in olive oil until translucent. Add chicken stock, potatoes, and carrots and bring to a boil until vegetables are tender crisp. Add cauliflower flowerettes, cabbage, salt, pepper and rosemary and simmer until all vegetables are cooked.

Remove rosemary and serve.

8 Servings

# Gazpacho

Each Serving: Cal: 125 Carb: 13 g Fat: 7 g Protein: 3 g Sodium: 711 mg Sugar: 8 g

3 tomatoes
1 large cucumber
1 small onion
1 red bell pepper
1 large can (48 oz.) tomato juice
1/4 cup olive oil
1/3 cup red wine vinegar
1 tsp. Tabasco Sauce
1 1/2 tsp. salt
1/2 tsp. pepper
2 cloves garlic, crushed

Peel and de-seed the tomatoes and cucumber. Clean and de-seed the bell pepper. In a food processor, puree the onion. Add the remaining vegetables and puree together. Add the remaining ingredients and mix well. Chill and serve cold. You may garnish with croutons or corn chips.

Optional to add grilled chicken breasts. Marinade chicken in lime juice, olive oil, salt and pepper. Grill chicken breasts until cooked through, cut into cubes and add to soup mixture.

6 Servings

# Quick
# Side
# Dishes

"Go vegetable heavy.
Reverse the psychology
of your plate by making
meat the side dish and
vegetables the main
course."
~ Bobby Flay

# Roasted Veggies

Each Serving: Cal: 197 Carb: 9.3 g Fat: 13.9 g Protein: 10 g Sodium: 362 mg Sugar: 3.8 g

4 golden potatoes, cubed
2 medium carrots, sliced
1 sweet potato, peeled and cubed
2 yellow squash, peeled and cubed
1 red onion, cut into wedges
1 clove garlic, minced
2 Tbsp. olive oil
2 Tbsp. balsamic vinegar
1 tsp. salt
1 tsp. pepper
1 tsp. basil
1 tsp. oregano
1 tsp. rosemary
2 cups goat cheese

Preheat oven to 400° F. Put all veggies into a large mixing bowl. Add garlic, oils and seasonings. Toss to evenly coat.

Distribute mixture onto a baking sheet. Bake for 35 minutes. Check that the veggies are the desired firmness.

8 Servings

*Family favorite*

Sides

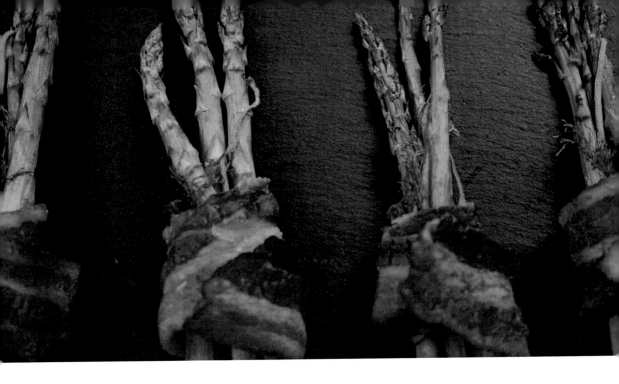

# Asparagus is Better in Bacon

Each Serving: Cal: 282 Carb: 36 g Fat: 11.9 g Protein: 9.5 g Sodium: 724 mg Sugar: 3.8 g

3 lbs. thin
asparagus
2 carrots
1 pkg. of fresh
baby dill
1/3 lb. bacon (12
thin slices)

Bundle 3 spears of asparagus with three thin slices of carrots and a spring of baby dill. Wrap each bundle with a slice of partially cooked bacon. Lay each bundle on a baking sheet covered with parchment paper. Bake at 325° F for about 15 minutes until bacon is crispy and vegetables are done.

12 Servings

# Caramelized Onion and Squash

Each Servings: Cal: 231 Carb: 17.7 g Fat: 18.3 g Protein: 3.5 g Sodium: 33 mg Sugar: 4.3 g

2 Tbsp. olive oil
2 onions, julienned
1 medium butternut
squash, diced
2 cloves of garlic
4 oz pecans,
chopped
1 Tbsp. fresh thyme

Heat 1 tablespoon of olive oil in large sauté pan. Add onions. Cook until onions are starting to turn brown (approximately 10 minutes). Add squash. Let stand for 5 minutes and then toss. Cook until squash is at desired firmness. Add garlic and thyme. Season with salt and pepper.

6 Servings

# Feta Potatoes

Each Serving: Cal: 282 Carb: 36 g Fat: 11.9 g Protein: 9.5 g Sodium: 724 mg Sugar: 3.8 g

Sides

8 red potatoes, cubed
2 cloves of garlic, minced
2 Tbsp. olive oil
2 Tbsp. water
3 Tbsp. lemon juice
1 tsp. dried oregano
1 tsp. dried thyme
1 tsp. salt
1/2 tsp. pepper
2 cups feta cheese, crumbled

Preheat oven to 400° F. In a large mixing bowl, add all ingredients and toss to evenly coat potatoes.

Pour mixture into a casserole dish and bake for 45 minutes. Check that potatoes are the desired firmness.

Add feta cheese and bake 5 minutes more.

8 Servings

*Family favorite*

# Mashed Cauliflower

Each Serving: Cal: 315 Carb: 6.8 g Fat: 25.8 g Protein: 15.2 g Sodium: 416 mg Sugar: 2.4 g

2 heads of cauliflower
4 cups of low-sodium chicken stock
1 8 oz. package of fat-free cream cheese
2 cups of low-fat sharp cheddar cheese, grated

Chop cauliflower into bite-size pieces and boil in chicken stock until tender. Drain off excess stock and add cheeses to the cauliflower. Stir and place in 9 x 13 inch baking dish.

Bake at 350° F until brown and bubbly.

10 Servings

*Great with turkey in place of potatoes; it's become a tradition for our holiday feasts.*
*-Jan*

Sides

# Sweet Potato Casserole

Each Serving: Cal: 312 Carb: 28 g Fat: 20.8 g Protein: 4g Sodium: 105 mg Sugar: 8.4 g

Filling Ingredients:
3 cups cooked sweet potatoes
2 eggs, beaten
1 Tbsp. vanilla
1/4 cup melted butter
1/3 cup milk
Topping Ingredients:
1/2 cup brown sugar, packed
1/3 cup flour
1/2 cup chopped pecans
1/2 cup butter, softened
1/2 cup oatmeal
1 tsp. cinnamon

To cook the sweet potatoes: Boil until soft, about 20-30 minutes and place in cold water. The skins will peel right off. Then mash with mixer or with hand masher.

For the filling: Mix the cooked and mashed sweet potatoes, vanilla, butter and milk. If you need to thicken, cook the mixture either on the stovetop or in the baking dish until it becomes a bit firm (it is best if it is thick like mashed potatoes and not runny like soup). Once the desired texture is attained, place in baking dish.

For the topping: Mix the topping ingredients until it's a crumbly mixture. Sprinkle the mixture over the top of the filling. Bake at 350°F for 30 minutes or until the filling is bubbling and hot.

10 Servings

*Family favorite*

Sides

# Fire-Roasted Corn

Each Serving: Cal: 117 Carb: 15.0 g Fat: 6.9 g Protein: 2.0 g Sodium: 152 mg Sugar: 2.4 g

8 ears fresh corn
2 Tbsp. fresh lime juice
1/4 cup olive oil
1 tsp. ground cumin
1 tsp. mild chili powder
1/2 tsp. fresh cilantro, chopped
1/2 tsp. salt
1/2 tsp. freshly ground black pepper

Heat grill to medium-high. Remove a few of the outer husks of corn. Gently pull back remaining husks, leaving them intact. Remove silk from corn.

Combine oil with all other ingredients and brush each ear of corn with oil mixture. Recover the ears of the corn with the husks that are still attached. Cook for 15 minutes, turning ears often.

8 Servings

*Family favorite*

# Parmesan Vegetable Casserole

Each Serving: Cal: 58 Carb: 5.1 g Fat: 3.9 g Protein: 1.9 g Sodium 56 mg Sugar: 2.3 g

1 medium head
cauliflower, cut
into florets
1/4 inch thick
2 Tbsp. butter
1/2 cup parmesan
curls or shreds
1/4 tsp. ground
black pepper

Preheat oven to 425° F. In a large pot, boil cauliflower until crisp but tender. Drain. Spray an 8 x 10-inch baking dish with non-stick spray. Lightly pack cauliflower in baking dish and season with freshly ground pepper, then dot with butter and sprinkle with the cheese.

Bake uncovered about 30 minutes or until lightly browned on top.

6 Servings

Sides

# Vegetable Fried Rice

Each Serving: Cal: 179 Carb: 30 g Fat: 3 g Protein: 6 g Sodium: 469 mg Sugar: 2 g

Cooking spray
1 tsp. vegetable oil
1 cup green onion, chopped
1 cup carrot, thinly sliced
1 medium garlic clove, minced
1 Tbsp. ginger, grated
2 eggs, lightly beaten
1 cup frozen sweet green peas, thawed
1 can water chestnuts, chopped
4 cups cooked long-grain brown rice
2 Tbsp. soy sauce
1 Tbsp. oyster sauce
1 tsp. sesame oil

Coat a wok or a large non-stick skillet with cooking spray, drizzle with oil and heat on medium-high until hot. Add green onions, carrot, garlic, ginger and bok choy. Stir-fry 3 minutes or until tender.

Make a hole in the middle of the vegetables by pushing them to the sides of the wok. Add beaten eggs to the center of the wok, stirring gently until set. Add peas and stir-fry 2 minutes. Add rice and stir-fry 2 minutes. Add soy sauce, oyster sauce and sesame oil.

Stir-fry until thoroughly heated.

8 Servings

# Greek Salad

Each Serving: Cals: 145 Carb: 10.7 g Fat: 10.0 g Protein: 4.4 g Sodium 217 mg Sugar: 5.3 g

Sides

1/4 cup apple cider vinegar
1/4 cup olive oil
1/4 cup lemon juice
1 tsp. salt
5 cloves of garlic, crushed
5 cucumbers, diced
5 tomatoes, diced
1/2 cup feta cheese

In a mixing bowl combine vinegar, olive oil, lemon juice, salt and garlic and mix well. Add cucumbers, tomatoes and feta and toss.

8 servings

# Cornbread

Each Serving: Cal: 229 Carb: 19.2 g Fat: 16.4 g Protein: 4 g Sodium: 276 mg Sugar: 1.7 g

1 cup cornmeal
1 cup coconut, rice or almond flour
4 Tbsp. agave
4 Tbsp. baking powder
1/2 tsp. xanthan gum
1 tsp. sea salt
1 cup coconut milk
1 egg
1/4 cup olive oil

Preheat oven to 350° F. Mix dry ingredients. Add liquids. Beat until smooth.

Bake in greased 8 x 8-inch pan for 25 minutes.

8 servings

*Thanks to Glenice Burton Powell for contributing this fabulous recipe via my Facebook page. The whole family loves it!*
*-Brenda*

# Delicious Main Dishes

"One cannot think well,
love well, sleep
well, if one has not
dined well."
~ Virginia Woolf

# Grilled Chicken Salad

Each Serving: Cal: 622 Carb: 29 g Fat: 42 g Protein: 35 g Sodium: 794 mg Sugar: 2 g

Polenta:
3 cups water
1 cup cornmeal
1/2 tsp. salt
2/3 cup parmesan cheese, grated
1/4 cup fresh basil leaves, finely chopped
Tomato Dressing:
1/4 cup white wine vinegar
1 Tbsp. Dijon-style mustard
2 cloves garlic, pressed
1/4 cup fresh basil, finely chopped
1/2 tsp. sea salt
1/4 tsp. ground black pepper
1/2 cup and 2 Tbsp. olive oil
2 plum tomatoes, seeded and finely chopped
1 lb. boneless, skinless chicken breasts
4 cups romaine lettuce, chopped
2 cups mixed baby greens, chopped
1 roasted red bell pepper, thinly sliced

Prepare polenta by bringing 2 cups of water to a boil in a medium-sized pan. In a small bowl, mix the rest of the water with the cornmeal. Stir mixture into the boiling water. Simmer over medium-low heat for 10 minutes, stirring often. Remove from heat and stir in cheese and basil. Spread polenta into a pie pan. Refrigerate until ready to use.

Prepare dressing by combining all ingredients and shaking until mixed. Cut chicken into cubes. Use 1/4 of the dressing to marinade the chicken and refrigerate for 30 minutes.

Place chicken on metal skewers and grill until chicken is cooked. Cut polenta into four squares and lightly brush both sides with olive oil. Grill polenta for about 4-5 minutes until polenta is crispy. Arrange pieces of polenta and chicken over the salad greens. Top with dressing and serve warm.

8 servings

# Chimichangas

Each Serving: Cal: 303 Carb: 2.5 g Fat: 9.5 g Protein: 46.4 g Sodium: 343 mg Sugar: 0.7 g

Main Dishes

2 lb ground beef
1/2 medium onion, chopped
1- 4 oz. can chopped green chilis (only use half of the can)
1- 7 oz. can Pace Picante salsa
1/2 tsp. salt
1/2 tsp. garlic salt
1/2 tsp. ground cumin
1 Tbsp. flour

Brown the ground beef with chopped onion, drain. Salt and pepper to taste. Add chopped green chilis, salsa, garlic salt, ground cumin, flour and stir.

Fill tortillas with 1/4 pound meat mixture. Put a teaspoon of olive oil in a pan and fry them without completely immersing in the oil. If you don't want the added fat of deep frying another option would be to bake them at 400° F until browned and crispy,

Top with guacamole, shredded cheese, sour cream, lettuce, tomato or salsa.

8 Servings

# Mexican Steak Dinner

Each Serving: Cal: 293 Carb: 7 g Fat: 15 g Protein: 34 g Sodium: 499 mg Sugar: 5 g

2 lbs. Round Steak
1 Tbsp. olive oil
1 clove garlic, chopped and mashed against cutting board
4 large tomatoes
1 8-oz can tomato juice
1/2 cup salsa (we use homemade)
1 onion, chopped
1/2 tsp. sea salt
1/4 tsp. ground black pepper

Cut steak into bite-size pieces and brown in olive oil. Salt and pepper to taste.

In blender, mix tomatoes, tomato juice, onion, salt, pepper, garlic and salsa.

Drain meat and add the blended mixture to the big frying pan. Simmer until warm throughout. Serve with warm, low-carb flour tortillas.

6 Servings

*Family favorite*

# Sweet Stuffed Picnic Peppers

Each Serving: Cal: 158 Carb: 8 g Fat: 4 g Protein: 23 g Sodium: 315 mg Sugar: 4 g

4 cups cooked chicken, shredded, chopped or even canned
1/2 cup low-fat mayonnaise
1/2 cup celery, chopped
1/4 cup green onions, chopped
2 Tbsp. fresh parsley, chopped
1/2 tsp. sea salt
1/4 tsp. ground black pepper
4 red bell peppers
8 leaves butter lettuce

Mix chicken with mayonnaise, celery, green onions and parsley. Add salt and pepper. Cut peppers in half, top to bottom. Remove core and seeds.

Place one lettuce leaf in each half pepper. Fill lettuce-lined pepper with ½ cup of chicken salad. Garnish with pickles or fresh radish slices.

8 servings

*Family favorite*

# Baked Salmon with Lemon & Dill

Each Serving: Cal: 268 Carb: 3.5 g Fat: 4.5 g Protein: 48 g Sodium: 257 mg Sugar: 0.3 g

4 fresh king salmon fillets, 6-ounces each
1/2 cup white wine
2 Tbsp. olive oil
Juice and zest of 1 lemon
2 tsp fresh dill, chopped
Salt and Pepper to taste

In a medium bowl, combine the wine, olive oil, lemon juice, lemon zest and dill. Stir until mixed well.

Lightly butter the pan and lay fillets in single layer. Pour the sauce over the fillets.

Bake at 350° F for 15 minutes until the fish is cooked.

4 Servings

Main Dishes

# Nine Layer Dinner

Each Serving: Cal: 334 Carb: 36 g Fat: 10 g Protein: 23 g Sodium: 446 mg Sugar: 5 g

1 lb. ground turkey
3 large tomatoes, chopped
1/4 cup water
1/4 tsp. red pepper flakes, crushed
2 Tbsp. fresh basil, chopped
1 1/2 cups low-fat cheddar cheese, grated
8 oz. Mastaccoli pasta
1 can refried black beans
1 red bell pepper, chopped
2 Tbsp. black olives, sliced
2 cups romaine lettuce, chopped
1 large tomato, chopped
4 Tbsp. fat-free sour cream

Fry ground turkey and drain. Add chopped tomatoes, water, pepper flakes and fresh basil. Cook breaking up the chopped tomatoes to form sauce.

Add 1/2 cup of grated cheddar cheese and the cooked pasta, and mix well. Divide pasta mixture onto 8 plates.

Top with remaining ingredients. Add spoonfuls of warm refried beans, sprinkle with cheddar cheese, bell pepper, black olives, romaine lettuce and tomato--and top off with 1/2 Tbsp. sour cream.

8 servings

# Garlic Chicken

Each Serving: Cal: 294 Carb: 10.0 g Fat: 13.1 g Prot: 33.1 g Sodium: 99 mg Sugar: 8.7 g

6 chicken breasts
8 garlic cloves, minced
2 Tbsp. honey
2 Tbsp. brown sugar
2 Tbsp. olive oil

Mix olive oil, garlic, honey and brown sugar together and coat chicken breasts evenly. In a frying pan on medium-high heat, cook chicken breasts for 4-6 minutes on each side.

6 Servings

Main Dishes

# Baked Tilapia

Each Serving: Cal: 181 Carb: 18 g Fat: 2 g Protein: 24 g Sodium: 99 mg Sugar: 3.2 g

4 - 4 oz fillets of fresh tilapia
3 carrots, thinly sliced
3 red potatoes, peeled and cut into strips
Fresh sprigs of rosemary
Fresh springs of thyme
1/4 cup green onion, chopped
1 lemon, juice and zest
1 lime, juice and zest

On a large, square sheet of tin foil, put one bundle of fresh herbs: one sprig of rosemary, thyme and green onions. Grate zest from lemon and lime and squeeze juice from both.

Add 1 filet of tilapia and one quarter of the vegetables (potatoes need to be par-boiled or they will be crisp.) Salt and pepper to taste.

Fold the foil around the fish, vegetables and herbs, creating a package. Bake at 350° F for 14 to 16 minutes. Open packets and serve.

4 Servings

# Blackened Chicken Salad

Each serving: Cal: 500 Carb: 36.9 g Fat: 14.2 g Protein: 55.8 g. Sodium: 2537 mg Sugar: 26 g

Dressing:
1 cup fat-free mayonnaise
1 cup Dijon mustard
1/2 cup honey
4 Tbsp. yellow mustard
4 Tbsp. white vinegar
1/2 tsp. paprika
Marinade:
4 cups water
1 cup lime juice
6 Tbsp. soy sauce
2 Tbsp. Worcestershire Sauce
Cajun Spice Blend:
1 tsp. sea salt
4 tsp. sugar
4 tsp. paprika
4 tsp. onion powder
4 tsp. black pepper
2 tsp. garlic powder
2 tsp. cayenne pepper
2 tsp. white pepper
2 Tbsp. butter
Salad:
Salad mix
6 chicken breasts
2 cups fat-free mozzarella cheese
2 cups fat-free cheddar cheese
1 tomato, diced
4 hardboiled eggs, diced

Make dressing by combining ingredients in a small bowl. Shake well to blend. Store in a covered container in the refrigerator until salad is ready.

Combine marinade ingredients. Add the chicken breasts to the marinade, cover and keep in refrigerator for several hours.

Heat grill to medium-high. In a small bowl, mix spices for the spice blend. Cover chicken breasts with blend and place on grill. Grill both sides until cooked. Spread cut chicken pieces on salad and serve with dressing.

6 Servings

*Note: Using low-sodium soy sauce and Worcestershire sauce will reduce the sodium to 1654 mg.*

# Salmon Packets

Each Serving: Cal: 193 Carb: 4.6 g Fat: 8.5 g Protein: 22 g Sodium: 306 mg Sugar: 1.7 g

8 - 9" squares of parchment paper
olive oil
4 Tbsp. butter, softened
1 sweet onion, cut in matchsticks
2 med. carrots, cut in matchsticks
4 lg. mushrooms caps, cut in matchsticks
1 tsp. fresh tarragon leaves, minced
16 fresh leaves
1 Tbsp. shallots
1 tsp. lime zest
3 lb salmon fillet
7 Tbsp. dry white wine
1 Tbsp. lime juice
1/4 cup clam juice

Melt butter in a saucepan. Add onions and carrots. Cover and cook over low heat until soft. Stir in mushrooms, minced tarragon, salt and pepper. Cover and cook for 4 more minutes.

Divide raw salmon into eight even portions and put one on each parchment circle. Split vegetables between each circle, and place portion on each filet and season with salt and pepper. Place 1 1/2 tablespoon of butter mixture on each salmon with vegetable pile.

Fold up packets and bake at 350° F for 30 minutes.

## 8 Servings

*Note: This is a fancy way to serve a delicious fish recipe. I often use it when entertaining or for special events, like Christmas.*
*-Brenda*

# Savory Chicken Satay

Each Serving: Cal: 270 Carb: 11 g Fat: 13.6 g Protein: 24.8 g Sodium: 610 mg Sugar: 6.3 g

1 envelope onion soup mix
1/4 c. olive oil
2 Tbsp. honey
2 Tbsp. sugar-free peanut butter
1 lb. chicken breast, sliced
12 skewers

In a large bowl, mix onion soup mix with olive oil, honey and sugar-free peanut butter.

Skewer the chicken. Generously coat skewers with the peanut butter mixture.

Bake at 350° F for 30 minutes.

6 Servings

Main Dishes

# Egg Souffle

Each Serving: Cal: 273 Carb: 23 g Fat: 21 g Protein: 17 g Sodium: 697 mg Sugar: 1 g

1 dozen eggs
1 tsp. salt
8 oz. sour cream
1 lg. can chopped green chilies
2 cups shredded cheddar cheese

Preheat oven 450° F. Beat eggs, salt and sour cream together. Fold in green chilies and cheese.

Pour into 9 x 13-inch baking dish.

Bake souffle for 45 minutes. Souffle is done when knife inserted in center comes out clean.

8 Servings

# Tomato Garlic Pasta

Each Serving: Cal: 332 Carb: 34.8 g Fat: 14.5 g Protein: 13.8 g Sodium: 452 mg Sugar: 0 g

4 lg. tomatoes, chopped
3/4 cup water
1/3 cup olive oil
1 t. basil
1 t. sea salt
1/2 tsp. black ground pepper
1/2 tsp. red pepper, crushed
12 large cloves garlic, minced or pressed
16 oz. pasta of choice
Grated Parmesan cheese

In a large frying pan, mince or press the garlic and lightly brown in olive oil. Add the tomatoes, the water, the seasoning and spices. Simmer uncovered for five minutes, stirring occasionally.

Cook pasta as directed on package and drain. Place in serving bowl and toss with sauce.

Sprinkle Parmesan on top of each serving.

6-8 Servings

*Family favorite.*

Main Dishes

# Stuffed Chicken Breasts

Homemade tomato sauce:
1 Tbsp. extra-virgin olive oil
3 large tomatoes, peeled and chopped
1 small onion minced
1 red bell pepper, minced
2 cloves garlic, minced
1/2 cup Cabernet Sauvignon or other red wine
4 Chicken breasts (about 1 lb.)
1 tsp. fresh rosemary, chopped
1/2 cup fat-free ricotta cheese
1/2 cup fat-free sour cream
1 egg, beaten
1 cup mozzarella cheese, grated
Fresh mozzarella cheese balls, sliced into 4 slices

In a saucepan, begin the tomato sauce by combining only the olive oil, onion and garlic. Toss until onion is translucent and add red wine. Add in tomatoes and bell pepper, and stir while heating. Cook for 20 minutes on low. As the sauce cooks down, it will thicken. Turn temperature to warm and prepare the chicken breasts.

Slit chicken breasts for stuffing, and set aside. Mix rosemary, ricotta cheese, sour cream, egg and grated mozzarella. Spoon 1/4 of this mixture into each chicken breast. Cover each stuffed breasts with tomato sauce and top with a slice of fresh mozzarella. Bake at 350° F for 50-60 minutes or until chicken is cooked through.

4 Servings

Main Dishes

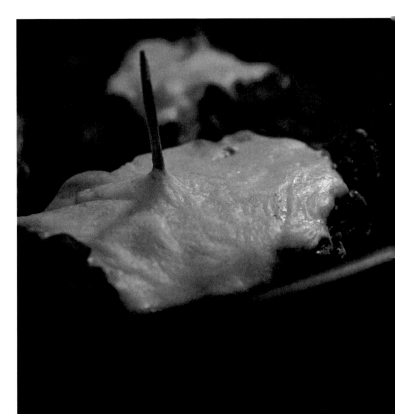

# Teriyaki Salmon

Each Serving: Cal: 321 Carb: 18.6 g Fat: 11 g Protein: 35.5 g Sodium: 861 mg. Sugar: 13.7 g

1/3 cup soy sauce
1/3 cup sake
1/3 cup mirin
2 Tbsp. honey
1 Tbsp. brown sugar
1 pineapple, cored and sliced
6 salmon fillets

Mix all marinade ingredients together. Pour 1/4 of marinade into a resealable bag and add pineapple circles. Place fillets into the remaining marinade. Allow pineapple and fillets to marinade for at least an hour.

Preheat grill to medium-high and grill fillets for 4-5 minutes on each side. Grill pineapple for 2-3 minutes on each side and put on top of salmon. Can be served over rice.

6 Servings

*Family favorite.*

# Chicken Lettuce Wraps

Each Serving: Cal: 406 Carb: 24.8 g Fat: 23.4 g Protein: 23.4 g Sodium: 822 mg Sugar: 12. 8 g

2 1/2 cups cooked chicken breast
5 butter lettuce leaves
1 cup grapes
1 cup celery, diced
1/2 cup slivered almonds
1 lg. can pineapple tidbits, drained
1 Tbsp. dried parsley, minced
1 cup mayonnaise
1/2 cup plain greek yogurt
1/2 tsp. sea salt

Mix grilled chicken breast (cut however you like) with mayonnaise, yogurt, salt and parsley and stir until chicken is well-coated.

Stir in celery, almonds, pineapple and grapes. Serve wrapped in butter lettuce leaves.

5 Servings

*Sometimes, to save time, I use canned chicken breast, which works great.*
*-Brenda*

Main Dishes

# Fancy, Crepe-like Pancakes

Each Serving: Cal: 125 Carb: 14.1 g Fat: 3.9 g Protein: 8.5 g Sodium: 253 mg Sugar: 5.8 g

1 cup buttermilk
1/2 cup cottage cheese
4 large eggs
2 Tbsp. sugar
1/2 cup flour
1 tsp. baking powder
1/2 t. baking soda

In a blender, add all ingredients (in order as listed). Use a Teflon frying pan to cook, and butter pan each time. Cook over medium heat. These are amazing topped with any kind of berries.

6 Servings

# Buttermilk Pancakes

Each Serving: Cal: 255 Carb: 27.2 g Fat: 13.4 g Protein: 6.6 g Sodium: 620mg Sugar: 2.9 g

2 cups flour
1/2 tsp. salt
2 tsp. baking soda
2 tsp. baking powder
2 eggs
2 cups buttermilk
1/2 cup butter

Preheat pancake griddle or Teflon frying pan. In a large bowl, sift together dry ingredients. Beat egg, buttermilk and melted butter in a separate bowl and add dry ingredients. Blend until well mixed. Pour 1/2 c. batter into pan per pancake.

8 - 10 Servings

Main Dishes

# Filet Mignon with Mushrooms

Each Serving: Cal. 477 Carb: 3 g Fat: 33 g Protein: 48 g Sodium: 169 mg Sugar: 1 g

4 - 6 oz. filet mignon
4 thin slices bacon
1 tsp. extra-virgin olive oil
3 green onions, finely chopped
2 cloves garlic, grated
1 cup white mushrooms, sliced

Preheat oven to 350° F. Wrap each filet with a partially cooked slice of bacon and set aside. Add olive oil to frying pan over medium heat. Add green onions and stir until softened. Add garlic and filets. Brown the filets on all sides and then place filets on a tray in the oven for desired doneness.

While the filets are in the oven, add mushrooms to the frying pan and fry about 2 to 3 minutes. To serve, place 1/4 of the mushrooms on a plate and add a filet mignon on top.

4 Servings

# Spaghetti Squash with Pork

Each Serving: Cal: 324 Carb: 24 g Fat: 17 g Protein: 20 g Sodium: 638 mg Sugar: 0 g

1 3-lb. spaghetti squash, halved lengthwise
1/2 cup grated Parmesan cheese
1/2 lb. Italian blend ground pork sausage
1/2 cup chicken stock
1/2 tsp. sea salt
1/4 tsp. ground black pepper
2 slices crisp bacon for garnish

Cut the uncooked squash in half and spoon out the seeds. Place squash halves, cut side down in a large microwave dish. Add 1 cup water and microwave until tender, about 15 to 20 minutes.

Using a fork, carve out the squash strands into a bowl. Toss with cheese, reserving some of the cheese for topping.

In a large skillet, cook sausage until no longer pink. Add chicken stock. Season with salt and pepper and serve over the spaghetti squash. Garnish with 1/2 slice crumbled bacon.

4 Servings

*Family favorite*

Main Dishes

# Halibut Tacos

Each Serving: Cal: 291 Carb: 26 g Fat: 9 g Protein: 26 g Sodium: 351 mg Sugar: 10 g

Marinade:
1/2 red onion, chopped
3 Tbsp. lime juice
1/2 tsp. salt
1/4 tsp. pepper
Yogurt-lime Sauce:
1 cup plain low-fat yogurt
1 Tbsp. lime juice
1/2 tsp. sugar
1/4 tsp. salt
1 tsp. chili powder
1 tsp. cumin
1 tsp. chipotle powder
Dash of hot sauce
Taco fillers:
1 1/2 lbs. skinless halibut fillets
8- 6" corn tortillas
2 cups shredded cabbage
2 avocado, cubed
1/4 cup fresh cilantro, chopped
Cucumber-Orange Salsa:
1 cucumber, peeled and diced
2 oranges, peeled and diced
1 jalapeno, chopped
Juice of 1 lime
2 Tbsp. fresh cilantro, chopped
2 Tbsp. red onion, minced
1/4 tsp. salt
1 tsp. honey

First prepare marinade. Place halibut in shallow dish and cover with marinade. Refrigerate 20 minutes.

Mix the yogurt lime sauce together, cover and chill. Next mix the cucumber-orange salsa and cover and chill.

Heat grill to medium-high. Spray cooking spray on a paper towel and wipe on grill. Cook the halibut 4 minutes on each side or until done. Portion halibut into 8 equal pieces. Warm the tortillas. Top each tortilla with approximately 2 ounces of fish, 1/4 cup of cabbage, 2 Tbsp. yogurt-lime sauce, 2 avocado slices and 1 1/2 teas. of cilantro. Serve with cucumber-orange salsa.

8 Servings (1 taco with yogurt- lime sauce and cucumber-orange salsa per serving)

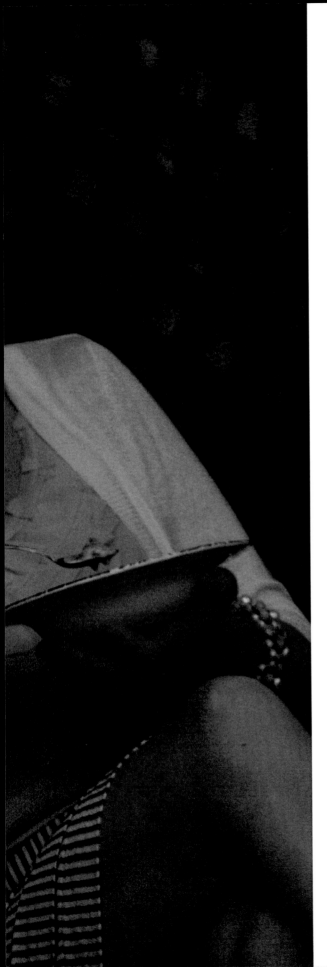

# Starters and Finishers

Starters and Finishers

"If more of us valued
food and cheer and song
above hoarded gold,
it would be a merrier
world."
— JRR Tolkien

# Mini Crab Cakes

Crab cakes: Cal: 100 Carb: 8g Fat: 1g Protein: 13g Sodium: 541mg Sugar: 0g
Aioli: Cal: 5 Carb: 1g Fat: 0g Protein: 0g Sodium: 54mg Sugar: 0g

3 cups lump king crab meat
1 1/2 cups Panko breadcrumbs
1/4 cup eggbeaters
2 Tbsp. fresh chives, chopped
2 Tbsp. fat free mayonnaise
1 Tbsp. Dijon mustard
2 tsp. Old Bay seasoning
1 tsp. lemon zest
Aioli:
3 Tbsp. low-fat mayonnaise
1/2 tsp. Cajun seasoning
1 1/2 Tbsp. lemon juice
1/4 tsp. Tabasco hot sauce

Preheat oven to 400° F. Line baking sheet with parchment paper. Combine crabmeat and breadcrumbs in a bowl.

In another mixing bowl, whisk egg, chives, mayonnaise, mustard, seasoning and lemon zest until blended. Add crab to mixture and stir.

Shape large spoonfuls of crab into small round cakes about 1 1/2 inches wide. Heat a skillet over medium heat and spray with cooking spray. Fry cakes one minute per side, until lightly browned. Transfer to a paper towel to absorb excess oil, and then transfer to baking sheet. Bake crab cakes for 10 minutes or until golden brown.

10 Servings (2 mini crab cakes with 1 tsp. of aioli per serving)

# Grilled Tomato Salsa

Each Serving: Cal: 90 Carb: 9 g Fat: 5 g Protein: 2 g Sodium: 168 mg Sugar: 4 g

4 tomatoes, cored
2 anaheim peppers
1 red onion, peeled and sliced
2 cloves garlic, peeled
Juice of 1 lime
1/2 tsp. sea salt
1/4 tsp. freshly ground black pepper
1/4 cup fresh cilantro, chopped
1 avocado, peeled & diced

On a hot grill or under a broiler, char tomatoes, peppers and onions. Peel peppers and remove seeds and veins.

In a food processor or blender, coarsely puree tomatoes, peppers, onions and garlic. Add lime juice, salt and black pepper. Cool salsa. Stir in cilantro and avocado. Taste and adjust seasoning for salt, pepper and lime juice. Serve with baked corn tortilla chips.

6 Servings

*Note: Nutrition information does not include chips.*

# Shrimp Dip

Each Serving: Cal: 77 Carb: 3 g Fat: 1 g Protein: 15 g Sodium: 578 mg Sugar: 2 g

1 1/2 lbs. (50-60) medium cooked, peeled shrimp with tails removed
1- 8 oz. pkg. fat-free cream cheese
3 Tbsp. lemon juice
3 Tbsp. fat-free mayonnaise
1 tsp. hot sauce
1/4 tsp. salt
1/4 tsp. black pepper
1/2 cup minced green onion, tops only

Chop shrimp and set aside, saving three whole shrimp for garnish (optional). Mix cream cheese, lemon juice, mayonnaise, hot sauce, salt and pepper. Stir in chopped shrimp and onion.

Cover and chill overnight.

Serve with low-fat crackers like pita chips or baked tortilla chips.

12 Servings

*Family Favorite*

# Meatballs

Each Serving: Cal: 372 Carb: 1 g Fat: 18 g Protein: 49 g Sodium: 207 mg Sugar: 0 g

1 ½ pound each of lean ground turkey and veal
2 cups grated Parmesan cheese
¼ cup eggbeaters
3 cloves garlic, grated
½ medium onion, grated
¼ cup fresh basil leaves, chopped

In a medium bowl, combine ground meats, cheese, egg, garlic and onion. Mix well and form into small balls. Fry in frying pan until golden-brown on all sides.

Place in oven at 300° F and bake until cooked through, about an hour. You may add a pinch of chili flakes to give it a little bite (optional). Form into 24 meat balls.

8 Servings (3 meatballs per serving)

# Cucumber Appetizer Sandwiches

Each Serving: Cal: 100 Carb: 11.3 g Fat: 5.5 g Protein: 3.4 g Sodium: 69 mg Sugar: 2.2 g

4 slices of whole wheat Bread
4 Tbsp. cream cheese, softened
1 package of sprouts
2 cucumbers, peeled and grated
1 avocado, sliced
Salt and pepper to taste

Spread 1 Tbsp. cream cheese over each slice of wholewheat bread. Add sprouts, grated cucumbers, sliced avocado and salt and pepper to taste. Cut into triangles and arrange on a platter.

8 Servings (2 triangles per serving)

# Chicken and Vegetable Cups

Each Serving: Cal: 198 Carb: 14 g Fat: 6 g Protein: 21 g Sodium: 308 mg Sugar: 3 g

2 lg. grilled chicken breasts, diced
1 large head of broccoli, cut into florets
8 sheets of phyllo dough
1 cup Monterey Jack, shredded
1 cup cheddar cheese, shredded
1/2 cup fat-free ranch-style dressing

Preheat oven to 350° F. Spray mini muffin tins with cooking spray and set aside. Lay 4 phyllo dough sheets out, one on top of the other. With a sharp knife, cut into 9 rectangles (approximately 4"x3".) Repeat for the remaining 4 sheets.

Lay the small rectangles into the baking tins. Bake 5 minutes in preheated oven. Allow cups to cool.

Mix chicken, vegetable, cheese and dressing together. Fill the 18 cups and bake for another 10 minutes, until bubbly. (Again, have fun with this recipe. Use vegetables that you like and that are fresh and in season.)

9 Servings (2 cups per serving)

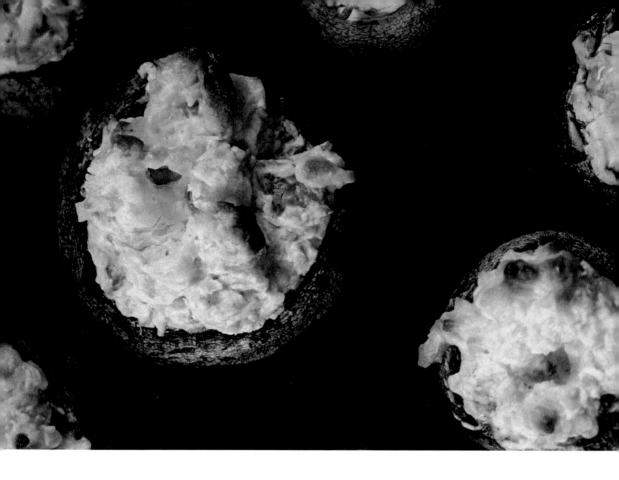

# Stuffed Mushroom Caps

Each Serving: Cal: 68 Carb: 5 g Fat: 2 g Protein: 9 g Sodium: 260 mg Sugar: 3 g

20 large fresh white mushrooms, cleaned
1 clove garlic, minced
2 Tbsp. green onion, finely chopped
2 Tbsp. grated Parmesan cheese
1/2 tsp. Tabasco sauce
3 slices bacon, chopped
2 ounces cooked, tiny shrimp
1/4 cup fat-free cream cheese

Heat oven to 400° F. Line sheet with parchment paper. Remove stems and place cleaned mushroom caps on the baking tray, stem side up.

Cook bacon, transfer to paper towels to absorb excess oil. Chop bacon.

In medium-sized mixing bowl, combine cream cheese, garlic, onion, cheese, hot sauce, bacon and shrimp. Mix well. Top mushrooms generously with the filling. Bake for 15 minutes until mushrooms are tender. Serve warm.

5 Servings (4 mushrooms per serving)

*Family favorite*

# Ted's Fresh Mex Mango Salsa

Each serving: Cal: 26 Carb: 6.0 g Fat: 0.1 g Protein: 0.5 g Sodium: 2 mg Sugar: 4.7 g

6 vine-ripened tomatoes
1 bell pepper (any color)
1/2 sm. can chopped green chilies
4 green onions (chopped)
1 mango (chopped)
1/2 t. garlic salt
Pepper to taste

Add all ingredients to salsa blender and blend (or do half and half if you don't have a big enough salsa blender). Serve with guacamole or just chips. (If you don't have a salsa blender, you can use a regular blender, but use it in "pulse" mode so that you don't liquefy it.) You can also hand chop everything.

8 Servings

# Garlic Shrimp

Each serving: Cal: 147 Carb: 5.4 g Fat: 6.0 g Prot: 17.8 g Sodium: 186 mg Sugar: 1.0 g

1 lb shrimp, peeled and deveined
2 Tbsp. olive oil
8 garlic cloves, minced
1 onion, chopped
1/4 tsp. ground cumin
1 lime, juiced
3 Tbsp. chopped fresh cilantro
salt and pepper to taste

In a medium-sized bowl, mix together the lime juice, cumin, salt and pepper. Add the shimp to the mixture and toss to evenly coat.

Allow shrimp to marinade for 15 minutes.

Over medium-high heat, saute the onion and garlic with the olive oil for about 5 minutes. Add shrimp and saute until shrimp are cooked, about 5 minutes.

8 Servings

# Grilled Peaches

Each Serving: Cal: 202 Carb: 42 g Fat: 5 g Protein: 3 g Sodium: 107 mg Sugar: 26 g

4 medium, ripe peaches, pitted and halved
2 tsp. cooking oil
1 Tbsp. sugar
1/4 tsp. ground cinnamon
Dash of hot sauce
2 and 2/3 cups no-sugar-added vanilla ice cream or low-carb vanilla ice cream
4 tsp. maple syrup
8 tsp. low fat granola

Prepare grill for medium heat. Combine the sugar, cinnamon and hot sauce. Sprinkle over peaches.

Using long-handled tongs, moisten a paper towel with cooking oil and lightly coat the grill. Prepare grill for indirect heat by using a drip pan. Place peaches over the drip pan and grill, covered, over medium heat for 2-3 minutes on each side or until tender.

For each serving, arrange one peach-half on a plate with 1/3 cup of ice cream. Drizzle with 1/2 teaspoon maple syrup and sprinkle with 1 teaspoon granola.

8 Servings

Starters and Finishers

# Jan's Tearoom Scones

Each Serving: Cal: 211 Carbs: 62 g Fat: 9 g Protein: 2 g Sodium: 101 mg Sugar: 43 g

2 cups all purpose flour
1/2 cup sugar
1 Tbsp. baking powder
4 Tbsp. unsalted butter, cold, cut into pieces
1/2 cup heavy cream

In a medium sized bowl, mix all dry ingredients. If you have a stand mixer with a flat paddle (like a KitchenAid), gently mix the butter pieces in until you get a nice crumble, otherwise cut the cold butter in using two table knives (or with your hands).

Slowly mix the heavy cream in until nice dough forms. You should be able to form the dough into balls/ovals. Bake on parchment paper on baking tray at 350° F for 20 minutes, until done in the center. Remove to a cooling rack.

10 Servings (1 scone per serving)

# Crumble Apples Cookies

Each Serving: Cal: 162 Carb: 16 g Fat: 10.9 g Prot: 1.1 g Sodium: 61 mg Sugar: 11.8 g

4 fuji apples
1/2 cup oats
1/3 cup pecans
1/3 cup brown sugar
1 tsp. ground cinnamon
1/2 cup butter, softened

Preheat oven to 350° F.

Mix together all ingredients except apples.

Core apples. Then cut them into thirds, creating circles. Scoop mixture onto each apple circle and place on a baking sheet. Bake for 15-20 minutes until apples are tender.

12 Servings (one cookie per serving)

# Crepes

Each Serving: Cal: 214 Carb: 31.3 g Fat: 6.1 g Protein: 7.8 g Sodium: 100 mg Sugar: 10.7 g

4 eggs
1 cup milk
1 Tbsp. melted butter
1 cup flour
1 Tbsp. sugar
Dash of salt
4 cups seasonal fruit

In a large mixing bowl, beat all ingredients together until smooth. Let stand for 30 minutes. Stir before using.

Lightly oil a Teflon frying pan and heat over medium-high. Pour ¼ cup of batter into hot pan and immediately spread to coat the bottom (creating a thin nice circle). Cook until the edges begin to turn brown and batter loses its shine, then flip.

To serve, fill each crepe with 1/3 cup fruit or berries and roll. Optional to add syrup.

6 Servings

*Try these crepes with goat cheese and blackberry jam as the filling. Delicious!*
*-Brenda*

# Cinnamon Orange Cookies

Each Serving: Cal: 90 Carb: 12.4 g Fat: 3.9 g Protein: 1.4 g Sodium 95 mg Sugars: 2.5 g

1 cup crisp rice cereal
2 cups flour
1 tsp. baking soda
1 Tbsp. cinnamon
2/3 cup sugar substitute
1/2 cup butter
2 Tbsp. grated orange zest
1/4 cup molasses
1/2 cup applesauce (no sugar added)
1 eggbeaters

Preheat oven to 350° F. Grind rice cereal in food processor to a fine powder. Place cereal in medium-sized mixing bowl and add flour, baking soda, cinnamon and sugar substitute. Mix dry ingredients, then add butter, zest, molasses, applesauce and eggbeaters. Mix well.

Drop onto parchment covered baking tray by the tablespoonful and bake for 12 minutes.

24 Servings (1 cookie each)

*Family favorite*

*Note: Optional Glaze: 2 Tbsp. fat-free cream cheese, 1 cup powdered sugar. With glaze each serving changes to: Cal: 112 Carb: 17.4 g Fat: 4.2 g Protein: 1.5 g Sodium 98 mg Sugars: 7.4 g.*

# Chocolate Treat

Each Serving: Cal: 154 Carb: 33 g Fat: 1 g Protein:3 g Sodium: 207 mg Sugar: 20 g

1 box of fat-free devil's food cookies (Snack Wells or store brand)
1 8 oz. pkg. fat-free cream cheese
16 oz. marshmallow fluff
1 pkg. Dream Whip
1 pkg. chocolate instant pudding mix
1 cup fat-free half-and-half

Place one cookie each into the bottom of a paper-lined cupcake or muffin tin that bakes 12.

In a medium-sized mixing bowl, blend cream cheese, marshmallow fluff and the chocolate pudding mix. Spread over cookie crust.

Mix 2 cups of fat-free half-and-half with the Dream Whip packages on high until stiff peaks form. Add pudding mix and blend on high until well mixed.

Spoon over each cookie and refrigerate.

12 Servings

# Lemon Mousse Mold

Each Serving: Cal: 183 Carb: 15 g. Fat: 11.2 g. Protein: 5.7 g. Sodium 107 mg Sugar: 5 g

Starters and Finishers

1 envelope unflavored gelatin
1/2 cup lemon juice
1 small pkg lemon gelatin (sugar-free)
1 cup pineapple juice
1 small pkg instant lemon pudding (sugar-free)
8 oz cream cheese
2 cups milk
2 cups lemon yogurt (sugar-free)
12 oz tub of whipped topping (sugar-free)
4 packets of sugar substitute
1/2 Tbsp. grated lemon rind
1/2 cup applesauce (no sugar added)
1 egg

Sprinkle gelatin over lemon juice and set aside.

In a small pan, dissolve lemon gelatin in boiling water. Now add unflavored gelatin mixture, dissolving well.

Soften cream cheese in microwave and put in blender. Add hot gelatin mixture and blend until smooth. Let cool.

In a large bowl, whisk or beat milk and pudding until well-blended. Using a whisk, blend in the rest of ingredients.

Pour into a sprayed bundt pan. Refrigerate overnight. Turn upside down on a large platter and decorate with fruit.

12 Servings

*Family favorite*

*New York Times & USA Today Bestselling* Author Brenda Novak has written more than fifty novels. She is also a mother of five, and there is nothing that turns a woman into a fighter more quickly than a threat to one of her children. When her youngest son was in kindergarten, he was diagnosed with Type 1 diabetes. She's spent the years since trying to juggle her career with the demands of providing healthy meals for her large and boisterous family, managing her son's diabetes care and raising money for research. To date, she's raised $2.5 million and is continuing her efforts with the sale of this cookbook, which includes her own personal recipes (all her healthy favorites) along with recipes collected from friend and co-author Jan Coad.

For more about Brenda's fundraising efforts, please visit www.brendanovakforthecure.org.

Thank you for participating in this worthwhile effort!

Made in the USA
San Bernardino, CA
05 July 2017